THIS JOURNAL BELONGS TO

_____

This Journal is for Your Soul

As one born to stand out, you've probably encountered people who would prefer you didn't make them uncomfortable. Others may have tried to shame, ridicule or silence you because your words and ideas might destabilise their worldview and trigger a crisis of consciousness. You may have already met people – and eventually, there will be many more such people – who are inspired by your spirituality, your strangeness, your uniqueness and your passions. It is not the thoughts and reactions of others, but your willingness to bear witness to your truths that matters most. Be willing to commit to your voice, your dreams and your insights with purposeful, passionate action. However, you cannot act on your visions or express your soul voice if you are unclear about what it is that is true for you.

Creating time and space to journal is important. This is an unconditionally supportive and sacred place where you can reflect and be absolutely honest about your light, your dark, your prayers and your fears. Before you put pen to paper, decide that your journal is going to be a zone of non-judgement, authenticity, spiritual blessings and healing. You have enough light in you to handle any darkness. As you explore your inner workings, you kick off a process of divine alchemy. Ask deeper questions and become aware of the pain that invokes divine assistance and the healing genius of the Universe.

This journal is your place to be real. Enjoy being you with all the intricacies and quirks that entails. There will never be anyone quite like you on this planet. The Great Divine is loving its experience of life as you right now. It always has and always will. In the challenges and the victories, the Divine is equally loving you, living you, being you and blessing you.

I believe you have found your way to this journal so your soul story can be discovered, told and creatively developed. A seed in you has sprouted and is swiftly pushing roots down into the earth. That soul plant is destined to become strong. It will break through the protective confines of the soil, reach towards the light and share divine beauty, nourishment, inspiration and more. When you work in this journal, you are tending to your sacred garden of soul.

You may work with words to diarise, write poetry or record dreams, meditations and messages from the spiritual worlds. You could use colour, shape and your favourite tools to create beautiful vision boards and collages throughout. I have expressed my own soul growth in these and other ways in the journals I have kept over the years. There are no limits to how you express yourself in this journal. It is made powerful by your choice to render it sacred.

If you have heard me speak or read some of my work, you will know I am prone to mixing up divinely inspired phrases with off-beat jokes, silliness and even swearing. To me, sacredness is an attitude. You can be real, messy and authentic and still be sacred. In fact, that is more sacred than any contrived image of what you think it should be. Taking those sorts of risks and being truthfully ourselves is our best chance of experiencing the unconditionality of divine love. It embraces all of you – your sacred rage, your grief and your wildly beautiful visions for yourself, your life and the world.

HOW TO USE THIS JOURNAL

I invite you to use this journal to open divine conversation between your body, your mind, your soul, your inner critic and your inner child – all of whom will need your love, strength and compassion. Maybe your future and your past selves will have a voice here too. If you already know the Divine loves you unconditionally, you may feel safe giving the Great Beloved permission to read what you write. You will feel the Divine response in your heart. Your every thought, reflection and question will be answered with healing, love, grace and encouragement.

This journal can become your trusted friend. When you need a place to go and be yourself, your journal is here for you. Human contact and divine relationship are so important. At their foundations is a loving, supportive, acknowledging relationship with yourself. This journal can help you build that. It can be a mirror into your soul, a tool through which you practice divine love for yourself and a reliable place to return to whenever your sacred rebel wants to absolutely, unconditionally, boldly and passionately express itself.

Ignite the holy fire of your spiritual life purpose. Fill these pages with whatever feels real for you. Do the creativity exercises when and how you wish – in groups, on your own, with your children – with the Divine as your creative guide.

Our creative energy honours our individuality. It is our birthright and a powerful source for personal healing and spiritual growth. To be disconnected from our creativity is exceptionally painful. Yet, many people believe it is normal and how we should be living! This is not true, and it is absolutely within our power to tap into our creativity at any time.

When we are disconnected from our creative energy, we do not honour the fullness and individuality of our being. We may feel our achievements lack meaning and try harder to fill the emptiness within. We might feel something is missing without quite knowing exactly what it is. To change all this, we need divine defiance. The sacred rebel within proclaims, "*I don't want to live this way. I dare to claim a different reality for myself, and it will happen!*"

Creativity generates confidence in our inner resources. It fosters a connection to something greater than the world of the five senses. You might think of it as the muse, inspiration or the Divine. Either way, creativity is a blessed connection with the Universe. It is an experience of divinity. It is no accident that the Divine is often called the Creator. When we dare to link our creativity with our spirituality – our connection to love, goodwill, peace and wisdom – we go from artist to healer, from creator to channel. We shine. This world is so in need of the unique light our beautiful spirits have to offer.

May the cage-rattler, feather-ruffler and boat-rocker within you be blessed, empowered and inspired to joyfully and alchemically rock this world into alignment with divine love. Namaste, beautiful wild one. Together we can shake and create a beautiful new world.

– *Alana*

A Note about the Healing and Creativity Processes

These are best done when you have set aside some time for yourself. They can be done relatively quickly or you can go deep and take longer if you choose. It is best to turn off mobile phones and other devices, keep the lighting soft and wear comfortable clothing. You are aiming for a space where you can go into your journey and not be distracted by the external world. These exercises can be easily adapted for small groups or children, for healing and creative development.

YOUR PRAYERS HAVE BEEN HEARD. THE CREATIVE INTELLIGENCE OF
OUR UNIVERSE IS STEPPING IN, SHAKING THINGS UP AND SORTING OUT
A SITUATION WITH GREATER WISDOM. LET GO AND HOLD ON TO YOUR
INNER SELF. ALLOW EVERYTHING ELSE TO BE REARRANGED BY THE
LOVING HAND OF LIFE.

SOMETIMES WE DON'T REALISE WE HAVE WINGS UNTIL WE LEAP OVER
THE EDGE OF WHAT WE KNOW AND BEGIN TO SOAR INTO A NEW LIFE.

TAKE ADVANTAGE OF A SHIFTING PATTERN IN YOUR LIFE BY LEAPING
INTO AN ENTIRELY NEW LEVEL OF CONSCIOUSNESS AND EXPERIENCE.
THIS IS NOT A TIME FOR SELF-DOUBT OR PLAYING SMALL. GET IN TOUCH
WITH THE COURAGE, BOLDNESS AND DARE-DEVIL WITHIN. TAKE THAT
STEP, BIG OR SMALL, INTO A FUTURE THAT IS BECKONING YOU FORWARD.

YOU ARE MEANT TO THINK AND DO THINGS DIFFERENTLY. AVOID THE
TRAP OF DOUBTING YOUR IDEAS ARE SPECIAL OR INTERESTING ENOUGH.
YOUR INSPIRATION COMES DIRECT FROM THE UNIVERSAL SOURCE.
BELIEVE AND RECOGNISE THE SIGNATURE OF GREATER INTELLIGENCE
WITHIN YOUR CREATIVE IDEAS.

SWEET SUCCESS, LIKE ABUNDANT HONEY, IS COMING YOUR WAY. COMMIT
TO AND DEVELOPMENT AN IDEA THAT YOU HAVE ALREADY HAD OR WILL
SOON RECEIVE. SEE IT THROUGH TO THE END. BEE-LIEVE!

Sit quietly and say: "I commit myself – body, heart, mind and soul – to that which will illuminate me with golden inspiration, and uplift me and those around me with love. I am open to receiving all the support and protection needed to truly honour this commitment. So be it."

HEALING AND CREATIVITY PROCESS:

Storm Wisdom
Overcoming Stagnancy and Blocks to Creative Breakthroughs

A thunderstorm is nature's way of gathering energy that needs to be released. With a release of tension, relief and freedom soon follow, often with a fresh perspective. This process is about breaking through and letting go so that creativity can follow.

You will need your journal, a pen and at least one layer of clothing that you can remove during the exercise. A scarf works well. Find a place where you can be alone and have some privacy, either inside or out in nature. If possible, raise your arms up, open to the sky. When you are ready, repeat the following:

Storms so wild
Storms of grace
I call your blessing
Into my heart now

May I release and let go
May I be revitalised and grow
I open up my heart
To you now

Storms of grace
I stand my ground
As I allow your magic
To cleanse and surround

Any outgrown energy
Which I no longer need
Anything which will sap
Or deplete rather than feed

Storms of grace
Merciful earth
With your help
I experience rebirth

When you have completed your declaration, place your hands in prayer at your heart and close your eyes for a moment. Breathe in and out and be aware of yourself, what you feel and what is happening in your body – from the top of your head to the soles of your feet.

Affirm out loud, "I am a divine creative being. I give permission for divine genius and healing to flow through me for merciful breakthroughs and spiritual renewal."

Play for a moment. Imagine, visualise, feel or pretend that Mother Nature is blowing a wild wind through your hair and over your skin. Close your eyes, tilt back your head and breathe it in.

Remove your layer(s) of clothing as you say aloud, "I release myself from the layers of the past! From whatever has constrained me!"

Place the clothing to one side and say, "Through divine creative genius, this is now so."

Play for a few moments, allowing your body to move as little or as much as it wishes, in whatever shapes or movements that feel good for you. You may wish to make sounds, sing, chant, grunt, hiss, roll about on the floor or plonk onto your bottom and sink into meditation. You may prefer to lay on your front, resting upon the earth.

When you are ready, be seated or stand comfortably, with your hands in prayer and say, "With gratitude for this healing, I now offer this thank you."

You can simply say thank you with your hands on your heart or in prayer. You might prefer to make an offering to the Divine in whatever way suits you. This can be through song, dance, drawing in the earth or by writing a love letter to the Universe and reading it aloud. Do whatever feels truthful for you at that moment. Notice what happens when you tune into your heart with gratitude for divine blessing.

THE SPIRITUAL ADVENTURER GOES THROUGH DARKNESS AT TIMES. IT
HAS A PURPOSE, LIKE WINTER. IT IS NOT IN ERROR OR THROUGH A LACK
OF CONSCIOUSNESS THAT YOU ARE HERE NOW. IT IS TESTAMENT TO YOUR
SPIRITUAL GROWTH AND CREATIVE PROCESS. JUST REMEMBER THAT THE
LIGHT OF THE HEART SUSTAINS YOU. IT EXISTS WITHIN YOU ALWAYS,
EVEN IN THE DARKEST DEPTHS OF UNKNOWN TERRAIN.

HONOUR YOUR PERCEPTIONS. EVEN IF IT CONFLICTS WITH WHAT
EVERYONE AROUND YOU IS SAYING OR THE SURFACE OF THINGS, TRUST
YOUR INNER GUIDE.

YOU WERE NOT BORN TO PLAY A SMALL ROLE IN LIFE. DREAM BIG – EVEN
IF YOU HAVE ABSOLUTELY NO IDEA HOW YOUR VISIONS MIGHT COME TO
PASS. SURRENDER THE DETAILS, TRUST IT WILL ALL WORK OUT AND KEEP
BELIEVING.

A MESSAGE FOR YOU FROM THE UNIVERSE: I HAVE RESOURCES YOU KNOW
NOT OF. IT IS SAFE TO TRUST IN MY WAYS FOR I LOVE YOU AND I AM
GUIDING YOU INTO ALL THAT IS RIGHTFULLY YOURS. NOTHING THAT IS
MEANT TO COME TO YOU WILL BE DENIED. IT IS SAFE FOR YOU TO LET GO.

LOVE YOURSELF ENOUGH TO HONOUR THE TRUTH, EVEN IF YOU FEEL
YOU ARE THE ONLY ONE DOING SO. SACRED REBELS NEED TRUTH LIKE
LUNGS NEED OXYGEN! TRUTH KEEPS THE ENERGY OF LIFE FLOWING. LIES
DAMPEN THE SPIRIT OF THE SACRED REBEL. WHEN THOSE WITH MORE
FEAR IN THEIR HEARTS AVOID THE TRUTH, YOU MUST NOT TURN AWAY
FROM IT.

THE SACRED WARRIOR WILL NOT ALLOW FEAR TO GAIN A STRONGHOLD
WITHIN THE HEART.

GET OUT IN NATURE AND COMMUNE WITH THE INFINITE. NO MATTER HOW
MANY TIMES, IN HOW MANY WAYS OR BY HOW MANY TONGUES UNTRUTH IS
SPOKEN, YOU KNOW WHAT YOU KNOW IN YOUR SACRED, REBELLIOUS HEART.
DON'T GIVE UP. OPEN UP TO HEALING. KNOW THAT THE TRUTH ALWAYS,
EVENTUALLY, PREVAILS.

State with confidence, "I now choose to forgive and release any person, situation or circumstance that has sought to shame me. I release this from my body, mind and heart, through unconditional love. I love, accept and claim all of me. I accept the unconditional and loving assistance that life wishes to send me for this journey now. I honour my creative power and my innate worth."

Say out loud, "I ask that all disappointing experiences of the past, that have led me to believe life is not trustworthy or that faith is silly or immature, be released from my mind, body and heart. I ask for help accepting that I can and will attract all that is needed into my life, at the perfect time and in the perfect way."

INNER RHYTHMS
Trusting Your Divine Timing

You cannot miss what you are destined for. Nor will you gain anything by trying to push yourself. When you allow your needs to be met in harmony with your own rhythms, you surrender anxiety and gain peace. Thus, you more gracefully open to your destiny at the right time.

You do not have to use music as instructed here if it is not practical. Find a space where you can move your body as freely as possible. This may involve curling up in a ball, dancing around the lounge room or running from one end of a field to another. Do your best to find a space where you can work with movement that feels suitable and supportive for you.

Play whatever type of music you feel you would like to listen to. Classical, death metal, rock, dance, folk, soul, meditation music or something else entirely is perfectly fine. You may like to create your own music with instruments or with your voice. You could listen to the sounds of life around you and add your own sounds to the mix. The best musical choice for this exercise is one that feels right for you. Choose music that matches, complements or responds to your current mood and state of mind.

When you are ready with your venue and your music, focus on your breathing and your body. Come into the here and now. How do you feel? What do you need to do right now? Do you want to move your arms, clench and release your feet, wriggle your jaw or vibrate the sides of your mouth and tongue? Perhaps you would like to shake off some energy and really move. Whatever movement feels best, go with it. It can be slight or exaggerated, fast or slow. Allow yourself to express through movement at whatever pace you need. It needn't match the music you chose. Enjoy at your own pace as you find your own sacred rhythm.

Say aloud, "I now release any unhealthy attachment to structures, routines and belief systems that prevent me from accessing and honouring my sacred inner rhythms. I love myself enough to give myself rest when needed, to trust my own timing and not feel forced or rushed. I believe in myself enough to take healthy inspired risks and action when it feels right to me. I trust in my inner rhythms. They are wise and helpful. Through unconditional love, so be it."

Feel free to keep moving, change music, meditate, rest, relax or write. Expressing yourself authentically in any way is going to free the flow of vital creative juices through your body, mind and soul.

REPEAT THIS STATEMENT THREE TIMES, WITH FEELING: "WHAT I WANT,
WANTS ME AND I AM NOW OPEN, WILLING AND CAPABLE TO RECEIVE IT
THROUGH UNCONDITIONAL LOVE."

Stand up, open your arms wide and hold them above your head for a moment. Imagine the beautiful light within you, shining out to the Universe through your open hands and heart. Imagine the Universe receiving that light and saying yes to you. If you are feeling cheeky, send a big, YES back to the Universe and laugh! That is all. That is enough. You are enough. So be it.

BE LED BY NATURE. TRYING TO CONTROL THE POWERFUL FORCES OF LIFE
IS LIKE TRYING TO FIT AN OCEAN IN A TEA CUP. ALLOW THE OCEAN TO
BE THE OCEAN AND LEARN TO SWIM IN IT. IT'S MORE INTELLIGENT AND
FAR MORE FUN.

You can outsmart old patterns and create new and improved relationships. You don't have to be drawn into drama or repetitive struggles. It's your time to become free from those struggles.

_____

_____

_____

_____

_____

_____

_____

_____

_____

_____

_____

_____

_____

_____

_____

_____

_____

_____

_____

_____

_____

BE AWARE OF YOUR ENERGY. WHAT DOES IT FEEL LIKE NOW? WHAT DOES
YOUR BODY WANT? DO YOU WANT TO MOVE, TO CURL UP, TO REST OR TO
DANCE AROUND THE ROOM WITH JOY? PERHAPS YOU WOULD LIKE TO
GIVE YOURSELF A REASSURING HUG? TAKE A MOMENT TO DO WHATEVER
YOU FEEL YOU NEED RIGHT NOW.

THE UNIVERSE LOVES YOU FOR YOUR UNUSUAL TAKE ON THINGS.
THE QUIRKINESS IN YOU DARES TO HONOUR THAT WHICH IS DIFFERENT
AND RENDERS THE IMPOSSIBLE, POSSIBLE. YOU MUST NEVER LOSE YOUR
ESSENCE AND BECOME DRY, SERIOUS, APPROPRIATE AND CONVENTIONAL.
NOT EVEN FOR APPEARANCE'S SAKE. YOU ARE HERE TO DEMONSTRATE
WHAT LIFE IS ABOUT.

HEALING AND CREATIVITY PROCESS:

Strange Creature
Unleashing Your Wild Divine Beauty

Nature never shies away from strange beauty. She allows for endless diversity and her sacred works are often peculiar and stunning. You live within her field of creative grace, as a specially created work that also creates!

For this process, you will need your journal and pen. If you are in the mood for a creative frenzy, then a box of dress ups, craft items, paper, canvas, paints, feathers or more could become part of your beautiful costume or piece of art. To begin, allow yourself to feel as though you are becoming soft and gentle in your mind, heart and body. Breathe easily. Relax.

Imagine the strangest and most beautiful creature you can. Bring it to life with colour and texture. Envisage the eyes, the body, the wings, the fur, the feathers … how bizarre can you get? What are its qualities, powers and characteristics? Be playful with the process.

If you find it difficult to visualise, you may like to write a description of your strange and beautiful creature or simply imagine what it would feel like. Does it have soft fur, sharp claws, feathery wings made of crackling, fizzing electrical currents or sensitive furry antennae with delicate eyes on the tips? Is it a strange flower that speaks? A tree that grows upside down? Whatever comes to you is just what is needed. Trust in your imagination – as subtle or as wild as it is – and let it speak to you.

After you have played with your imaginings, complete your healing process with this declaration:

"I am supported through the shock of the new, I accept the beauty in all that is foreign or strange to me as I know it is bringing me gifts, wisdom, life experience and creative inspiration. Through unconditional love, so be it."

Imagine your words soaring into the far recesses of the universe. Complete this process by playfully recreating the vision of your strange and beautiful creature self. Use costume, art, poetry, music, dance, sound or a combination of whatever feels most liberating, fun and energising to you in this moment.

PLACE YOUR HANDS AT YOUR HEART IN PRAYER AND CLOSE YOUR EYES.
BOW YOUR HEAD TO YOUR HANDS AND IMAGINE, SENSE OR PERCEIVE
A BEAUTIFUL GOLDEN LIGHT POURING DOWN FROM THE CENTRE OF
THE UNIVERSE INTO THE TOP OF YOUR HEAD. IT FLOWS SLOWLY DOWN
THROUGH YOUR HEAD, INTO YOUR HEART, ALL THE WAY DOWN THROUGH
YOUR BODY AND OUT THROUGH THE SOLES OF YOUR FEET.

HOW BRAVE YOU ARE! YOU ARE DIVING FOR LIGHT. IT CAN BE SO MUCH
SIMPLER TO SEEK LIGHT IN THE HEAVENLY, IN THAT WHICH IS BLISSFUL,
SWEET, LOVING AND KIND. TO LOOK FOR THE LIGHT IN THAT WHICH
IS DARK IS AN ADVANCED TASK THAT ONLY A REBELLIOUS AND BRAVE
HEART WILL ATTEMPT.

IT IS OKAY TO BECOME SOFTER. FEEL THE ENERGY OF WHAT YOU WISH TO
ATTRACT INTO YOUR LIFE. ACT (AS MUCH AS YOU CAN) AS THOUGH YOUR
WISHES HAVE ALREADY ARRIVED. DOING SO IS NOT FANTASISING, DAYDREAMING
OR FAILING TO LIVE IN THE REAL WORLD. IT IS WORKING WITH THE FEMININE
ART OF MANIFESTATION THROUGH GENTLE BEING AND ATTRACTION.

YOUR HEART IS BIG ENOUGH TO DREAM FOR YOURSELF AS WELL AS FOR
A NEW HUMANITY. IMAGINE A WORLD THAT IS HEALED WITH RESPECT,
UNDERSTANDING AND A COMMUNITY THAT FOSTERS LIFE. EVEN THE
DREAMS THAT RELATE TO YOU ALONE WILL CONTRIBUTE TO THE
GREATER GOOD. THAT IS THE NATURE OF YOUR HEART.

PRONOUNCE WITH FEELING: "I NOW BREAK ANY CONTRACT I HAVE EVER MADE WITH ANOTHER, CONSCIOUSLY OR UNCONSCIOUSLY, THAT HAS GIVEN THEM POWER OVER ANY PART OF ME. I NOW CHOOSE TO DIRECTLY PERCEIVE MY INNER BEAUTY. I TURN WITHIN WITH KINDNESS AND COMPASSION AND SEE MYSELF THROUGH EYES OF UNCONDITIONAL LOVE."

THE UNIVERSE LOVES A BOLD SPIRIT. ONCE YOU TAKE A STEP, IT WILL RUSH
TOWARD YOU LIKE AN ENTHUSIASTIC AND CHIVALROUS LOVER. DOORS WILL
OPEN. A GENTLE HAND WILL GUIDE YOU FORWARD. YOU WILL BE PROVIDED
WITH ALL YOU NEED TO TAKE THE NEXT STEP.

ANY CONFUSION OR UNCERTAINTY YOU HAVE FELT IS GOING TO PASS. YOU WILL
BE LEFT WITH CLEAR INSIGHT. THE STORIES YOU HAVE BEEN FEELING, FEEDING
YOURSELF OR TELLING YOURSELF MAY END DIFFERENTLY TO HOW THEY NOW
APPEAR. THIS MAY SURPRISE YOU. HOWEVER, THE VISION THAT IS COMING TO
YOU WILL BE MORE TRUTHFUL AND FREEING.

YOUR DREAMS ARE BEAUTIFUL AND NEEDED, BUT THE WORLD NEEDS
YOUR CREATIONS AS WELL. GET THEE TO THY DESK! THY EASEL! THY
COMPUTER! WORK, BEAUTIFUL DREAMER. DON'T JUST DREAM, CREATE!

YOU ARE SHEDDING. IT MIGHT BE AN IDENTITY, A SOCIALLY ADMIRED
RELATIONSHIP OR A STATUS SYMBOL SUCH AS A CAR, HOME OR SUBURB.
YOU ARE SHEDDING BECAUSE REGARDLESS OF APPEARANCE, THOSE OLD
FORMS WERE TOO CONSTRICTING FOR YOUR SPIRIT.

HEALING AND CREATIVITY PROCESS:

HUNTER
Reclaim Your Power

An empty cup cannot quench the soul thirst of anyone! Making the needs of others more important than your own helps neither you nor them. Learning to love, respect and care for yourself is the basis of all healthy and supportive relationships. This process will help you release misplaced guilt, shame or unworthiness that prevents you from meeting your needs. It is time to break the habit of self-neglect and cultivate true self-love.

Find a space where you have some privacy and room to move. Somewhere with soft lighting can help you tune out the day-to-day world and place your attention on yourself and your inner world. Turn off the phone and other distractions if you can. Give yourself the permission and the time to go within. Have your journal and pen ready. You may also like to have your *Sacred Rebels Oracle* or other divination tool ready for this exercise.

Get comfy and relax as you imagine, perceive, feel or pretend there is a deep, indigo night sky above you and a full moon shining. There is stillness.

For a moment, there is peace. Then you hear wings moving through the air and see an owl pass in front of the moon. There is grace and unwavering focus in the movement. There is absolute certainty and precision. Feel the power and natural ability of this animal to navigate with strong unwavering instinct.

Now imagine that the owl is with you. It might be sitting above you on a tree branch or by your feet. Feel your vision become sharp and your hearing acute. You are able to see, hear and sense the truth, even when it is obscured by lies, manipulations, unconsciousness or deception. You will be a successful hunter for truth. You will not fall prey to illusion.

Say, "I am willing to accurately perceive the truth in whatever life situation is now helpful for my spiritual growth and creative awakening. I feel empowered to commit to myself and my path, without fear or holding back. I receive this vision through unconditional love. So be it."

Rest and in your own time, just open your eyes. Were there impressions, thoughts or intuitions that occurred to you as you rested? Jot them down, even if they seem irrelevant or silly or incomplete.

If you wish, you can go deeper into this process by working with a divination tool, such as an oracle deck or pendulum. If you don't have any tools, you can use a natural oracle. For example, gaze at cloud formations or a candle flame in a relaxed state and record what you see, sense or feel. You can ask specific questions of your oracle or go deeper into your insights from the first portion of this healing and creativity process by saying, "Through unconditional love, I ask what is most helpful for me to know now?" Continue to use your tools and record your answers in your journal through drawing, prose, poetry or whatever feels best for you.

Don't discount your sense of things. When something occurs to you, don't dismiss it. Affirm to yourself, "With unconditional love, I will be inspired as to how to creatively and consciously deal with this. So be it."

You have completed this healing and creativity process. As the process above is a trigger for deeper work and awareness, notice the impressions, intuitions and thoughts that occur to you over the coming days or weeks. Be sure to add them to your journal as expressions of your inner wisdom, guidance and creativity.

IF YOU ARE CONFUSED ABOUT YOUR MOTIVES, YOUR ACTIONS OR WHO YOU ARE BECAUSE OF WHAT OTHERS ARE SAYING, STEP BACK. IN YOUR QUEST TO BE A RESPONSIBLE PERSON, YOU MAY UNINTENTIONALLY BE TAKING ON THE FEELINGS OF OTHERS. DO NOT MISTAKE A REFLECTION FOR THE TRUE YOU. ACKNOWLEDGE YOURSELF. DO SO AND BE FREE!

WHAT REALLY MATTERS IS THAT YOU HEAR YOUR OWN VOICE. OTHERS MAY OR MAY NOT BE ABLE TO RECEIVE IT. WHEN YOU HEAR YOUR VOICE, YOU ARE CONNECTED WITH YOUR HEART'S TRUTHS. YOU WILL KNOW WHEN IT IS RIGHT TO REMAIN CONNECTED TO ANOTHER OR TO WALK AWAY FOR A TIME SO CAN FOLLOW YOUR OWN HEART'S GUIDANCE.

DO YOU KNOW HOW MUCH JOY THE UNIVERSE GAINS FROM BEING ABLE
TO GIVE TO YOU? DELIGHT IN WHAT YOU RECEIVE. OPENLY EMBRACE
A GIFT. BE HAPPY AND THE UNIVERSE IS FULLY RECEIVED BY YOU. IN
THIS SPACE, THERE IS JOYFUL COMMUNION BETWEEN YOU AND LIFE.
ENERGY FLOWS MORE FREELY AND MAGIC HAPPENS.

YOU ARE A SACRED WARRIOR — A DEFENDER OF THE HEART. THE SACRED
WARRIOR MUST NOT HEED THE DANGEROUS VOICES THAT SAY, "OH, STOP
BEING SO SENSITIVE! STOP MAKING SUCH A BIG DEAL OUT OF THINGS!"
LOVE IS THE BIGGEST DEAL THERE IS. WHAT ELSE IS WORTH BEING SO
SENSITIVE ABOUT? THE SACRED WARRIOR HONOURS THE TASK OF BEING
MORE FAITHFUL TO LOVE, THAN TO ANYTHING ELSE.

It is time to bring something in for you. To receive and be received. You are being offered a chance for restoration now, to feel nourished, cared for and loved. Accept it! You deserve it.

In every creative process, in every birth, in every opening to something new, there is vulnerability. This vulnerability is natural and appropriate, like the foal's unsteady legs. Those legs will become remarkably powerful in time, but a process of growth and maturity must take place first. There will be some wobbly first attempts. It cannot be any other way.

THERE IS NO NEED TO PUSH QUITE SO HARD TO RECEIVE WHAT IS
NATURALLY COMING TO YOU. YOU PUSH BECAUSE YOU ARE UNCERTAIN
OF SUCCESS. RELAX AND HAVE FAITH IN YOURSELF. SUCCESS WILL COME
RIGHTFULLY, ACCORDING TO GREAT AND LOVING WISDOM.
HAVE PATIENCE.

DON'T MAKE THE MISTAKE OF BELIEVING THAT WHAT YOU NEED LIES WITH
ANOTHER OR IS YET TO APPEAR. YOU DON'T NEED AN ARMY OF RESOURCES
TO MOVE AHEAD. HOWEVER, WHEN YOU DO MOVE, YOU MAY FIND RESOURCES
SUDDENLY BECOME APPARENT. YOU ARE MORE PREPARED THAN YOU REALISE.
YOU HAVE EVERYTHING YOU NEED TO TAKE THE NEXT STEP IN YOUR LIFE.
FROM THAT STEP, ALL ELSE WILL FLOW.

FEEL HONOURED BY THE LESSONS IN YOUR LIFE. STAY HUMBLY CENTRED
IN YOUR POWERFUL, REBELLIOUS HEART THAT REFUSES TO BE CONQUERED
BY FEAR AND REMAINS FAITHFUL TO LOVE. ALL WILL BE WELL. YOU HAVE
DIVINE LOVE ON YOUR SIDE.

SURRENDER ANY FEARS YOU HAVE OF APPEARING EXOTIC, UNUSUAL,
ECCENTRIC OR BIZARRE. ALLOW YOUR IDEAS OF BEAUTY TO BECOME
EVEN MORE INSPIRED AND OPEN, SO THAT YOUR UNIQUE, WILD SELF CAN
BE FELT, EXPRESSED AND EXPERIENCED.

WHEN WE ARE WHO WE ARE IN TRUTH, WE ATTRACT THE SUPPORT, PROTECTION AND ENERGY THAT WE NEED TO THRIVE. YOUR POWER COMES FROM ALIGNING YOUR OUTWARD SELF WITH YOUR INNER TRUTH, NOT WITH THE CONSENSUS.

DESTINATION NOW
Trusting Your Divine Journey

You are on a journey. Yes, it is an internal journey but the physical expression of this journey is going to become increasingly important to the fulfilment of your destiny in this lifetime. This exercise aims to help you help yourself by empowering the Universe to be the tour guide for your life journey. When you get into this mindset, the Universe can hook you up to the best possible people, places, situations and opportunities for you to fulfil your destiny and have the most beautiful and fun time in the process. This exercise is also good when you really need to get out of a rut, out of your head and relax enough to get things flowing again.

Say aloud, "I believe in myself. I trust myself. I have faith in the unfolding journeys of my life, both internally and out in the world. Even in the face of the unknown, I know that positive energy surrounds me and I am protected. Through unconditional love, I am supported and assisted to take each step as needs be so that my great creative life journey can be all that it can be. The Universe helps me in all ways now – the timing, the protection, the right situations and the best opportunities all coincide in my heart, mind and life with perfectly divine synchronicity. I am blessed!"

You may like to complete your healing process with a quick dance around the lounge room feeling joy in your heart and lightness in your step. If you are feeling more adventurous, you can add this prayer to your morning routine so that the entire day ahead becomes a journey with the Universe as your guide. Say it before a holiday, a day out, a trip to the beach or a visit to the supermarket! Experiment. Learn to feel what it is like to have the Universe as your ally. As you do this, you will come to notice how the timing of your day unfolds perfectly. Things will fall into place and life will not be such a struggle all the time. You will have your challenges but you will also have much more support, guidance and help.

YOU WANT BIRDS TO FLY UNDERWATER. YOU WANT TO MAKE
POSSIBLE WHAT OTHERS SAY CANNOT BE. YOU ARE A RADICAL
DREAMER. SACRED REBEL, YOU BRING THE LIGHT OF A MORE
POSITIVE FUTURE TO THIS WORLD.

In life and the creative process, there is a need for wild storms. Storm wisdom brings things to a head and clears the way. Allow energy to be freed from a pattern that has had its day. It is ready to become something new.

GROWTH WILL COME WHEN YOU LET GO OF THE NEED TO HIDE FROM
THE WORLD. THE WONDER THAT LIES WITHIN YOU WILL FLOURISH IN
THE LIGHT OF DAY. TRUST YOURSELF. LET THE REAL YOU COME OUT
FROM BEHIND THE VEIL. IT IS SAFE TO BE SEEN.

DISPENSE WITH YOUR RELIANCE ON YOUR OLD WAYS OF NAVIGATING
LIFE. YOU HAVE OUTGROWN YOUR FAMILIAR METHODS. YOU MUST FLY BY
THE SEAT OF YOUR PANTS AS YOU EXPERIMENT WITH NEW WAYS
OF BEING. LIFE WILL SHOW YOU THE WAY.

TRUST THAT YOU CAN STEP INTO SOLITUDE WITHOUT BEING CONSUMED
BY LONELINESS. IT IS TIME TO RECONNECT WITH YOURSELF. YOUR
LEVEL OF SELF-LOVE IS GROWING AND THUS YOUR ABILITY TO LOVE
CONSCIOUSLY AND HEALTHILY IS INCREASING. KEEP DOING YOUR WORK
BECAUSE IT IS WORKING FOR YOU — AND OTHERS TOO.